FOCUSED

A SPIRITUAL GUIDE TO LIVING A FOCUSED LIFE

LATASHA POWE

CONTENTS

INTRODUCTION

Have you ever heard someone say, "Stay Focused, Let's Focus, be focused," etc.?... So how do we do this? And why is it so important? Why is it important to God? Did you know that God cares about what we focus on? Mainly this book places our attention back on the main things, which are God and His purpose for us. Most of us have read in the bible how Peter walked on water. But many of us have a limited understanding of how his focus kept him from sinking. I know what you are thinking, it was Jesus that caused him to walk on water, but I have a different viewpoint. It was Jesus's command for Peter to step out, but Peter's focus made the journey until he began to focus on his surroundings. We can receive instructions and obtain valuable information, but it is not until we "apply" what we have been given that causes things to happen! In Matthew chapter 14, verses 25-31 of the King James Bible reads, shortly before dawn Jesus went out to them, walking on the lake. When the disciples saw him walking on the lake, they were terrified. "It's a ghost, they said and cried out in fear. But Jesus immediately said to them; "Take courage! It is I. Don't be afraid." "Lord, if it's you," Peter replied, "tell me to come to you on the water." "Come," he said. Then Peter got down out of the boat, walked on the water and came toward Jesus. But when he saw the wind, he was afraid and beginning to sink, cried out, "Lord, save me!" Immediately Jesus reached out his hand and caught him. You of little faith," he said, "why did you doubt?" Why did you think you could not do it? Or why did you lose FOCUS?

The bible gives us many clues as to what we should pay attention to. Let's examine one of my favorites in the book of Isaiah. Just before the semicolon in Isaiah 43:19 (AMP), it says, "Listen carefully, I am about to do a new thing, Now it will spring forth; Will you not be aware of it?" I have read this often and it has never resonated within me as it has the past few years. The Lord spoke this to me in a still small voice. Yet when He spoke this verse, the words were just a little different. I heard it this way, listen carefully, I am doing a new thing, it will happen so fast that if you are not focused, you will miss it! How powerful! So how do I do this? How do I stay focused, so I do not miss what God is doing? Often, fear or uncertainty steals attention from our goals, desires, and even our destiny. When we concentrate on a particular outcome, fear loses its power to take away our focal point position. Satan has used subtle tools such as multitasking, overloaded schedules, and projects to keep us busy, but not productive, to work his plan. It is a simple, almost unnoticeable tool the adversary uses to make sure we are distracted while his plans to steal, kill and destroy go unnoticed. I pray that as you read each page, you recognize the little foxes in your life that are often disguised as busyness.

In this book, I share a personal insight, scriptures, and prayers that have helped me overcome distractions. *Jesus* says, in John Chapter 10 verse ten, *the thief cometh not, but for to steal, and to kill, and to destroy: I am come that they might have life, and that they might have it more abundantly.* When we are not focused, the thief, our adversary, the devil is stealing from us, killing our purpose in hopes of destroying our lives! But, No More! We are taking our power back by taking charge of our thought life and living on every word that proceeds from the mouth of God.

But, before we go any further, let us pray… Father, we thank you that you have made us in your image and likeness. We repent for being absent from your word and in your presence and being more present and attentive to the things of this world. Thank you for another chance, new mercies, and grace. From this day forward, please lead and guide us into all truth and shed light on the areas of our lives we give more focus to than we should. In Jesus' name, Amen.

FOCUS ON PURPOSE

In the book of Philippians, of the King James Bible, Chapter 4 verse 8, Paul writes, Finally, brethren, whatsoever things are true, whatsoever things are just, whatsoever things are pure, whatsoever things are lovely, whatsoever things are of good report; if there be any virtue, and if there be any praise, think (focus) on these things. Think is a synonym for focus. If we used it in the last part of the verse, we just read and replace it with focus. It should be obvious why focus is important to God. Look at a few of Webster's definitions for focus, (1) is *a state or condition permitting clear perception or understanding, and* (2) is a center of activity, attraction, or attention. Our lives follow what our attention is on. Jesus's life was one of the greatest examples. In John 6:38, Jesus says, "For I came down from heaven, not to do mine own will, but the will of him that sent me." Everything Jesus did was the will of God. How did he do this? He kept His father's will as his focus! Although he did many things, Jesus had one assignment, to do the will of the father that sent him.

The world's perspective of doing multiple things equals productivity, but I beg to differ. Productivity without focus equals many things being done but not effectively. Imagine where you would be if you're driving but not paying to where you were going? You would probably not end up at your desired destination. An article called 12 Surprising Reasons Multitasking Doesn't Work in Health Magazine gives the outcomes of several studies on multitasking, and here are a few from that article. Experts say that switching between tasks can cause a 40% loss in productivity and cause more errors if one or more of your activities involve critical thinking. The article also states that multitasking requires a lot of "working memory," or temporary brain storage. And when all that memory is used up, it can take away from our ability to think creatively (the University of Illinois at Chicago, Research). God is the creator of everything in the universe. As His children, we are to imitate him in creativity, and performance. This is one reason what we focus on is important to Him.

Focus Scriptures

Psalms 32:8 KJV I will instruct thee and teach thee in the way which thou shalt go: I will guide thee with mine eye.

Proverbs 3:6 KJV In all thy ways acknowledge him, and he shall direct thy paths.

Psalms 143:8 KJV Cause me to hear thy lovingkindness in the morning; for in thee do I trust: cause me to know the way wherein I should walk; for I lift my soul unto thee.

Focus Thought

Daily I put my trust in you. Your wisdom shall be my guide. I commit every work and plan before me to your care. Every decision I make, I trust your guidance. I no longer lean to my understanding, and I acknowledge you in all my ways. Your way is right.

Prayer Focus

Father, I thank you for leading me into all truth and righteousness. Forgive me for not seeking your counsel in every area of my life. Thank you for a renewed mind and perspective. Busyness will no longer deceive me. In Jesus Name, Amen.

FOCUS ON THE VISION AND PRIORITIZE THE PURPOSE!

It is prominent to focus and prioritize our God-given vision and purpose. Our purpose can be found only in seeking God. It is the reason we were created from the beginning. Our creator is the only one that can reveal our purpose. It was determined long before we even existed. Let us read Jeremiah 1:5 *before I formed thee in the belly, I knew thee, and before thou camest forth out of the womb I sanctified thee, and I ordained thee a prophet unto the nations.* This purpose has not changed! As born-again believers, we should not only say what God says, but we should also see what He's said manifest. We tell the good news, the gospel, and we live the way He has exemplified in His Word!

Without a target, we have no true direction for our lives. When focused on the main thing (purpose), we are not driven away by all the minor things. Meaning we do not choose just to be busy but choose to progress and see results. Those that are focused are persons of stability and wise in determining what to pursue, invest or build.

Remember, if we seek the kingdom of God first, His way of doing things, all the other things will fall into place and be available to us (see Matthew 6:33).

God has led me to study the traits of the eagle, and this is another one of those times. Recently I came across an article on the 7 Principles of an Eagle (September 2008 elutosin.com, Emmanuel Oluwatosin).

Let us look at principles 6 and 7.

Principle 6: The Eagle Prepares for Changes: When ready to lay eggs, the female and male eagle identify a place high on a cliff where no predators can reach. The male flies to earth and picks thorns and lays them on the crevice of the cliff, then flies to earth again to collect twigs which he lays in the intended nest. He flies back to earth and picks thorns, laying them on top of the twigs. He flies back to earth and picks soft grass to cover the thorns. When this first layering is complete, the male eagle runs back to earth and picks more thorns, lays them on the nest, runs back to get grass on top of the thorns, then plucks his feathers to complete the nest. The thorns on the outside of the nest protect it from possible intruders. Both male and female eagles participate in raising the eagle family. She lays the eggs and protects them; he builds the nest and hunts. During the time of training the young ones to fly, the mother eagle throws the eaglets out of the nest. Because they are scared, they jump into the nest again.

Next, she throws them out and then takes off the soft layers of the nest, leaving the thorns bare. When the scared eaglets again jump into the nest, they are pricked by thorns. Shrieking and bleeding, they jump out again this time, wondering why the mother and father who love them so much are torturing them. Next, the mother eagle pushes them off the cliff into the air. As they shriek in fear, the father eagle flies out and catches them up on his back before they fall and brings them back to the cliff. This goes on for some time until they flap their wings. They get excited at this newfound knowledge they can fly.

Preparing the nest teaches us to prepare for changes; the preparation for the family teaches us that active participation of both partners leads to success; the being pricked by the thorns tells us that sometimes being too comfortable where we are may result in our not experiencing life, not progressing and not learning. The thorns of life come to teach us we need to grow, get out of the nest, and live on. We may not know it, but the seemingly comfortable and safe haven may have thorns.

Principle 7: The Eagle Knows when to Retire: When an Eagle grows old, its feathers become weak and cannot take him as fast as he should. When he feels weak and about to die, he retires to a place far away in the rocks. While there, he plucks out every feather on his body until he is bare. He stays in this hiding place until he has grown new feathers, then he can come out. We occasionally need to shed off old habits & items that burden us without adding to our lives.

What an interesting read! Maintaining our focus is not always comfortable, but necessary for growth and progression. At every stage in our lives, there will be a time of refocusing. The key is to know when. God's wisdom can assist us greatly in discerning these times.

Our relationship with God is important to our success in following His plan for our lives. The more intimate the relationship, the closer you are to your destiny. You ever heard someone say, "I was so focused on what I was doing; I didn't realize you were talking to me?" This is the same attitude we must take on! Why? Because many distractions come to lead us off the main path. I believe that we are in a time where we do not have time to waste. Every second of the minute, of every hour in our day is vital to staying the course to end cycles of fruitless days, weeks, months, and years. Through prayer and self-discipline, along with perseverance, we can do it!

Focus Scriptures

Proverbs 4:26 AMP Consider well and watch carefully the path of your feet, And all your ways will be steadfast and sure.

Isaiah 30:21 KJV And thine ears shall hear a word behind thee, saying, This is the way, walk ye in it, when ye turn to the right hand, and when ye turn to the left.

Proverbs 3:5-6 KJV Trust in the Lord with all thine heart; and lean not unto thine own understanding.6 In all thy ways acknowledge him, and he shall direct thy paths.

Focus Thought

Daily I commit my works to God, that they may succeed and be established. I guard my heart so my path is straight, and I am confident in where I am headed.

Prayer Focus

Father, thank you for your tender mercies that are new every morning. I know your voice, and I will not follow doctrine contrary to your word. Thank you for teaching me to meditate upon your word day and night. Forgive me for not seeking your direction for my life in times past. In Jesus' name, Amen.

ARE YOU STILL IN LOVE?

Remember the first time you laid eyes on your spouse, your newborn baby, or even those new shoes? Oh, the joy and warmth you felt can easily fade by life changes and challenges, and time itself. Therefore, staying focused is so vital. If you only marry for beauty, there will be many times you will be disappointed. In our marriages, we need focus. Why? In marriage, sometimes, we take one another for granted, forget to say I love you, or give one another compliments. Yes, this happens! Because life has a way of doing what it does, going on, and whether we take time to smell the roses or not. When the newborn ages into a hormonal teenager, will we still be as loving and patient as we were when they were helpless infants? The many challenges of life can cause us to forget the bigger picture.

The environment we live in should be created for us to thrive. When we do this, we are mindful of what we allow our ears to hear, our eyes to see, and what we speak out of our mouths. We must do things on intent. No one fails on purpose, and although most success is planned, it was also done with intention.

God is the same God we were on fire for and zealous about at the beginning of our salvation. He will not change through grief, loss, sickness, and other trials and tribulations we may face. You must stay the course, no matter what happens. God isn't the cause of our difficulties, but He can use them to cause us to triumph!

Focus Scriptures

Revelation 2:4 (KJV) Nevertheless I have somewhat
against thee, because thou hast left thy first love. 5
Remember therefore from whence thou art fallen, and
repent, and do the first works; or else I will come unto thee
quickly, and will remove thy candlestick out of his place,
except thou repent.

Focus Thought

Each day I commit to setting time aside to pray and talk to God. I purpose to participate in worship on Sundays and in my home and heart daily. I will stay connected to the vine, which is Jesus, by reading and studying the word of God daily.

Prayer Focus

Father, I repent for not staying connected to you through prayer, worship, and your word. As I reflect on who you are, I turn from those ways and things that keep us apart. You loved me before I even existed. Thank you. In Jesus' name, Amen!

TUNNEL VISION

What is tunnel vision? And how can it benefit me? There were many definitions to define tunnel vision, but overall, I preferred the British Dictionary definition. The British Dictionary defines tunnel vision, as a condition in which peripheral vision is greatly restricted; or narrowness of viewpoint resulting from concentration on a single idea, opinion, etc., to exclude others. This question was asked to me, how is your ministry going? I was taken back. The question was not what area of ministry do you serve in or what do you do in ministry, but was the ministry God placed inside of me being fulfilled? Wow! This got me thinking. Not that we are not supposed to care about the ministry in which we are a part of and or serving in, but we cannot let the ministry inside of us die either. God has placed His visions, dreams, and purpose in us so His Kingdom can be manifested in the earth. But how do we get to the point where we shut out all the noise of opinions, thoughts of others, and even ourselves, to hear God about the matter, to receive His instructions as to what steps to take? When you think about the answer to this question, so many thoughts arise, and a little urgency. Picture yourself driving through a tunnel, and there are no other cars, you can see the small glimpse of light, but it is still far away. You know that you are coming out, but it is still a journey to the light. While you are in the tunnel, your attention is on the glimpse of light you keep getting closer and closer to, and nothing else matters. That my friend is called, tunnel vision! There will be many circumstances, trials, and even times when our accomplishments will come as distractions, but as you develop tunnel vision, your focus will remain.

Focus Scriptures

Colossians 3:2 AMP Set your mind and keep focused habitually on the things above [the heavenly things], not on things that are on the earth [which have only temporal value].

Proverbs 4:25 ESV Let your eyes look directly forward, and you gaze be straight before you.

Hebrews 2:1 ESV Therefore, we must pay closer attention to what we have heard, lest we drift away from it.

Focus Thought

Daily I set my mind on God's purpose and plan for my life and doing things His way!

Prayer Focus

Father, I give you access to every thought, idea, and suggestion that enters my mind. Everything that comes in my mind that exalts itself against the true knowledge of God and His plans about my life is destroyed in the name of Jesus and captive to the obedience of Jesus Christ. Amen.

ATTENTION SEEKERS, BEWARE!

Attention seekers cannot maintain a life of focus. Why? Because they will always depend upon other people's opinions of them. This stunts growth and creativity and places you under unnecessary pressure. God's creativity cannot flow freely when someone has subjected themselves to what other people think about them. One thing we should remember is that flesh is never satisfied; it knows no limits. What does God say about you? What does He say about your destiny? Do you know who you are aside from your career or title? When you know who you are; having the attention of others is not a concern. The saying, "one should serve not to be seen, but seen serving" is such a powerful statement. The danger in being an attention seeker is that the focus is always on you, not God or others. God loves to commune with us and for us to willingly commune with Him. We must keep the Holy Spirit as our focus in everything we do. God loves us with all our flaws, insecurities, and shortcomings, but He desires to make us better if we submit all those concerns to Him.

One of the greatest deliverances I have experienced is that of being free from the expectations and opinions of others. I have learned to embrace mistakes, failures, and missing the mark. But what did I learn from those mistakes, failures, and falling short? I have learned that the power is in getting up again and again. Choosing not to stay trapped in condemnation or defeat, determines how long you stay there. It was good I failed. Mistakes are only mistakes if you never learn from them, but they can become milestones and tools when you do. Am I saying to embrace the falls, mistakes, etc.? Yes, I am! It is your fuel in life. The key to staying delivered and victorious is to know that you are! We cannot always see the end but, ask yourself, what would you do if you knew you could not fail? Your answer would be everything you have ever wanted to do. Perhaps you would dream impossible. Remember, Matthew 19:26, states, With Men this is impossible; but with God all things are possible.

Focus Scripture

Matthew 6:1 (KJV) Take heed that ye do not your alms before men, to be seen of them: otherwise ye have no reward of your Father which is in heaven.

Proverbs 24:16 (NKJV) For the righteous falls seven times and rises again, but the wicked stumble in times of calamity.

Philippians 3:13 (NKJV) Brethren, I do not count myself to have [a]apprehended; but one thing I do, forgetting those things which are behind and reaching forward to those things which are ahead,

Focus Thought

Today, I will not give attention to all that is going on in my life, but instead, I will think of others. I understand that if I am always thinking of myself, that I will miss the things and people that God will place in my path so someone may see and experience Him! Holy Spirit helps me to be more like you, as you came to earth as a servant and not to be seen serving.

Prayer Focus

Father, we repent so thinking of ourselves more highly than we should have and giving so much attention to ourselves. Thank you for allowing us to see that only giving attention to ourselves will not bring you glory. We thank you for opening our spiritual eyes and ears we may be more attentive to your purpose for our lives and that we are becoming better builders of your kingdom. In Jesus' name, Amen!

TO FOCUS OR NOT TO FOCUS, IS THE QUESTION

Here is where it may get a little tricky. We all know (well most of us) that we just cannot think of ourselves only. But when do we focus on ourselves, and when do we take the time to concentrate on others? Do we wait until the kids are older and off to college? When we have obtained that promotion or made a partner in the firm? Discerning these times requires wisdom we can only God can give. His insight and timing can be the GPS we can use to tell us when, where, how, but only if we accept it. Our father knows this life is full of multitasking and busy schedules. He can navigate us through it all.

I used to get everything done in a day! If I completed the entire task at hand, I would be happy. Can you believe that? I was basing my happiness on the daily task I finished. Wow! I know it's funny right, but I had to learn that my happiness was not predicated upon completing my everyday household duties or assignments at work. My focal point had to shift. We wear ourselves out mentally and physically during the day that by the time we get home to our families, we are too tired to help the children with their homework or simply ask our spouse how his/her day went. We cannot do it all! I know you may think you can, but you cannot. There will be times in our lives when things will not go as planned and we must learn to be ok with that. We must solely depend on the Holy Spirit to lead and guide us through the journey of life and teach us balance. *To Focus or Not to Focus is the Question*, the choice is yours. The word of God is our GPS and is available to us for guidance on this journey called life.

Focus Scriptures

Matthew 19:26 (KJV)

But Jesus beheld, them and said unto them, with men this is impossible; but with God all things are possible.

John 16:13 (NIV)

But when he, the Spirit of truth, comes, he will guide you into all the truth. He will not speak on his own; he will speak only what he hears, and he will tell you what is yet to come.

Focus Thought

Today with intention, I purposely watch my words because I frame my world by my words. I am careful about what I hear and see and any negative seeds planted by words, thoughts, and ideas; I abort and uproot them now, in Jesus' name. I will only nurture and give birth to the seeds and plans that God placed on the inside of me. I will water and feed those seeds with the word of God and prayer. I am victorious because the same spirit raised Christ from the dead. I will not be defeated in my mind; therefore, I take authority over distractions and anything that will try to steal my focus.

Prayer Focus

Father, we thank you for leading and guiding us into all truth. We thank you for a reset in our thinking and because we believe, we now know that all things are possible with you. Help us to keep our minds clear and free of the clutter of things and thoughts not of you and cause us to remember the power of our words and that what we focus on, our lives will follow. Help us keep the main thing, the *main thing*. We thank you for helping us to realign our will to yours. We pay attention to what we focus on. Thank you for a mindset to press on and the grace to begin again with a new, godly perspective. Thank you for revealing the unseen and the recovery of time wasted. Holy Spirit, we welcome you into every area in our lives we did not before. Today is a new day and we embrace it! We will remain FOCUSED! In Jesus' name, Amen.

ENCOURAGEMENT FROM THE AUTHOR

When I wrote this devotional, I had no idea that I would be challenged in so many areas of my life to maintain my focus. This devotional began three years ago! I came to the Lord when I was 25 years old. I have served and am currently serving in ministry for 17 years. I have served single, married, as a mother, a student, employed and unemployed, as a teacher and an administrator. Every assignment requires a different strategy for keeping yourself focused and being productive. At numerous times I felt stuck. One of my greatest fears was the sacrifice of taking on too much. I never wanted to be too exhausted, where I did not have time for my husband or to read to my children at bedtime. The biggest fear was that I did not want to fail. Many times, I would try to choose what I would invest my time in because of this fear, but God always chose for me. He taught me through trial and error that if you keep the main things, the main things, I could give attention to more than one thing at a time, and it would not be at the sacrifice of my marriage, family, career, or myself. If we continue to give our attention to all of life's many diversions, we will never move into what God has for us.

Believe it or not, everyone will not like what you do or say, how you serve, how you parent, etc., even when doing it the way God has told you to! This is where developing that tunnel vision (p.15) becomes your tool to use to stay the course and not be moved by everything and everyone's opinion of you. You will get hurt, used, and misused, be tolerated instead of celebrated, uninvited, mishandled, and misjudged, misled, overlooked, counted out, and on and on, but be encouraged. Jesus experienced everything we will ever encounter, and He pressed on to do the will of the Father. Keep going! Stay Focused!

Made in the USA
Las Vegas, NV
02 October 2021

31475149R00020